Abigail Scott Duniway

Abigail Scott Duniway

PATH-BREAKING WRITER

In 1895, as she launched a new journal dedicated to bringing equal rights to all the women of America, Abigail Scott Duniway had already been a key figure in the national woman's movement for over two decades. And during those years, dramatic changes had been taking place. As she wrote, "though 'Liberty for all the inhabitants of the land' has not yet been secured, we have made much permanent progress, and now nobody doubts our ultimate success" ("Salutatory" *PE* 16 Aug. 1895). At the beginning of Duniway's career, women's rights were severely restricted. With few exceptions, marriage brought an end to a woman's legal identity altogether; it meant entering into a state of civil death. A wife had no official existence apart from her husband's. Under the principle of coverture (in which a woman is said for legal purposes to be covered, or overshadowed, by her husband's presence), the two were made one, and that one was the masculine partner in the enterprise. In that era, married women in most of the U.S. couldn't sign contracts, had no title to their own earnings or to property, nor any claim to their children in case of separation or divorce (Flexner, *Century* 7-8). But by the end of 1896, Idaho and Utah would join Wyoming and Colorado as full suffrage states, and enormous strides would be made on multiple fronts in the equal rights battle. The age of the New Woman, who had "recently discovered herself in sufficient numbers to awaken the alarm of her adversaries," was dawning—and she had in large part been conjured by the imaginations of her pioneer foremothers, who had dared to dream, and to express those dreams in writing, as did the woman her contemporaries referred to as "Mrs. Duniway."

The story of how a former Illinois farm girl rose to become an influential author and spokesperson for equal rights is one that parallels those of many other western women whose experiences in a new land helped them to break free of conventional norms and redefine the boundaries of "woman's sphere." After immigrating overland to Oregon in 1852, the girl known in her youth as Jenny Scott, and later as Abigail Scott Duniway, had played the roles of pioneer homesteader, school teacher, and milliner, and had given birth to six children. But this was just a prelude to her later career, during which she would write 22 novels, become an influential editor and nationally renowned lecturer, and serve as vice president of the National Woman Suffrage Association (NWSA). For over 40 years, in the face of scorn, she avidly worked, with pen and voice, to promote legislation that would give women the same status as men. When in 1914, a year before her death, she published her autobiography and named it *Path Breaking*, she could not have chosen a better title. The new path she trod at the end of the old Oregon Trail was one that transformed the future for millions of women.

Duniway's contributions to the fight for equality were made on many fronts. She was directly involved in the political arena. As a spokesperson for the National Woman Suffrage Association, she lectured extensively, was often invited to address state legislatures, and worked tirelessly behind the scenes building relationships with men of influence whose votes would ultimately determine the outcome of her efforts. But, although for many decades Duniway was remembered predominantly as a political figure given to fiery oratory, her writing was actually of wider influence than her speeches. The many volumes of her weekly newspaper, the *New Northwest*, published in Portland, Oregon (1871-1887), and her later effort, *The Pacific Empire* (1895-1898), which contain most of her literary output, tell the story of how the west was won for women. In her "Editorial Correspondence," Duniway tells stirring tales of her travels throughout the Pacific Northwest, and of her even more momentous cross-country journeys. She describes the people she met and the places she ventured to in a very striking fashion, often with acerbic humor. In her serialized novels, she fictionalizes the scenes and people encountered in her actual adventures, and incorporates them into lengthier narratives that dramatically expose women's oppression with the end of motivating readers to reject the status quo, rise up, and bring about change.

Duniway's writing leaves a unique record of life in the old west as seen from the vantage point of an ardent feminist. Her stories and columns inspired disenfranchised, often isolated women, and turned them into the vanguard of a new generation that would make the west a bastion of hope for the rest of the nation. In this region, laws were passed granting women voting rights and other important legal protections far in advance of the rest of the country. Wyoming Territory, in 1869, was the first place where women were allowed to vote in all elections. The other states of the Rocky Mountain west followed suit, and by 1914, the remainder of the westernmost states had adopted women's suffrage as well, whereas only one state in the rest of the country, Kansas, had done so. When equal suffrage was enacted nationally in 1920, many western women had been voting for over a quarter of a century.

What happened in the vast landscapes of the American west that led to such momentous change? When we examine Duniway's path-breaking writing we find a trail to follow in seeking the answers. We discover that, as in her own case, at the end of their journeys west many women found themselves released from the stricter customs of the east, and took advantage of the opportunities afforded by a new, restless country where there was so much work to be done in the settling of a new region that unusual contributions became the norm. They also demanded civil rights out of self-defense, reacting to the unsettled conditions that endangered their already tenuous status, such as the loss of female community and family ties in sparsely populated regions, and the loosening of conventions censuring men's worst behaviors. As we leaf through Duniway's writings, we find the way in which changed conditions, occurring at an auspicious moment in history, emboldened women to claim equal rights to "life, liberty, and the pursuit of happiness," and made the men who labored beside them more likely to realize that their counterparts were by no means lesser beings.

The periodicals edited by Duniway were influential beyond what mere circulation figures suggest. Sources report that, at its peak, the *New Northwest* could boast only an approximate 3,000 subscribers. However, pass-along readership was high in the nineteenth century, particularly in frontier communities; populations were small, and the publication's subscribership included many (in the region, and across the nation) in positions of influence. Susan B. Anthony read Duniway's novels aloud to her elderly mother, who enjoyed them with relish. As Martha M. Solomon reflects in *A Voice of Their Own: The Woman Suffrage Press, 1840-1900*, "newspapers and journals became the ties that bound women together and made them into a social movement" (14). Periodicals such as the *New Northwest* helped to forge a political movement as well.

Duniway's narratives tell a revisionist story of women's roles in the early west that predates what are normally considered to be revisionist offerings by a century. In "Feminism, Women Writers and the New Western Regionalism," Krista Comer observes that in the late twentieth century writers have turned "conventional western tropes—the West as land of fresh starts, western landscape as regenerative resource—toward feminist ends," and in doing so "remake both feminist and western discourse" (23). And yet, Duniway's work often makes that of her latter-day successors seem tame, and reminds us that feminist progress has not followed the consistently upward trend that popular opinion erroneously believes it has.

At the time Duniway wrote her earlier novels, the west was still wild and woolly in the greater part of the eastern imagination, but she wrote of it as the *new* New England—freer, with a brighter future, harbinger of a greater civilization than ever the east could create. In her autobiography, she spoke of how "the free, young, elastic West" had compelled "the women of the older states, crystallized with constitutions hoary with the encrustations of long-vanished years," to look to the west "for the liberties they cannot get at home" (*Path Breaking* 167). This aspect of the west's history is chronicled superbly in all of Duniway's writing.

FROM ILLINOIS FARM GIRL TO VOICE OF EQUAL RIGHTS

When she crossed the plains in 1852 on her way from Illinois to her new home in Oregon, 17-year-old Abigail Jane Scott (called "Jenny" by her family) followed an already well-trodden path. By July 14 of that year, 18,765 men, 4,270 women, over 5,000 children, close to 8,000 horses, 5,000 mules, 75,000 head of cattle, 23,000 sheep, and a total of 7,516 wagons had passed Fort Kearny, Nebraska, heading west along the Oregon Trail (Scott 226). So many immigrants thronged the way that as the season progressed it became harder and harder to find grass for the animals, water sources were polluted, and a cholera epidemic raged out of control. Death became an everyday experience. The Scott party, originally numbering 52—including Jenny's parents, eight sisters and brothers, relatives, neighbors, and teamsters—lost six members en route, and a grave-littered roadside testified that such tolls were not uncommon (Holmes 13-17; D. Duniway 21-38). Jenny's adventures along the Oregon Trail, shared by many others, were painful, but also liberating. In combination with what she observed in the new life found at her destination, these experiences would lead the outspoken teenager to blaze a trail of her own as a persuasive advocate for women's rights.

Born in a log cabin in rural Tazewell County, Illinois, on October 22, 1834, Jenny Scott would not seem to have had much chance of achieving public success. Often suffering from "severe physical afflictions" as a child, she attended a "little log school house about a mile distant [. . .] at intervals" (*Path Breaking* 34), and at the age of 16, studied for five months at "an apology for an academy" about 20 miles from her home (qtd. in Moynihan 11). As she reflected in 1904, "If it be true that I am a 'literary woman' [. . .] I must have been so born; for certainly I was never blessed with the advantages of education, or the association among literary people which is supposed to be a necessary accompaniment of success" ("How I Became A Literary Woman").

Nevertheless, as was the case with so many of that time, her scant formal education had been generously augmented by extensive reading. Many newspapers entered the Scott family home, and young Jenny soaked in all she could, including Horace Greeley's *New York Tribune*, which publicized all of the major "reform movements of the day, from Fourierism to Graham's vegetarianism to female dress reform," and the early woman's rights publication, the *Lily*, edited by Amelia Bloomer. As noted by her biographer, Ruth Moynihan, "Abigail Jane Scott was anything but isolated from the currents of change and reform that were surging throughout the country in her youth" (10). Bursting with all she absorbed, and feeling compelled from an early age to express herself on paper, Jenny began to write poetry, and one of her verses was even published in the local *Illinois Journal*, although no copies survive (11).

But Duniway's literary career really begins with her family's 1852 trek overland to Oregon. At the journey's outset, Jenny, the second eldest child, was appointed family scribe by her father, John Tucker Scott (1809-80), and she recorded the history of their migration—made on foot, by horseback, and in an ox-drawn wagon—in her "Journal of a Trip to Oregon" (published in 1986). This is an often-eloquent diary, filled with enthusiasm for the magnificent landscapes. Her detailed description of geographic features, although sometimes trite in comparing odd landforms to "ruins of magnificent structures of the Old World" ("Journal" 64), brings the scenes to life. As Kathleen Boardman notes, it was difficult "for emigrants to describe the unfamiliar lands through which they were passing. [. . .] A common technique is to compare the unfamiliar with the familiar"—which for many, such as Jenny, meant places they had read of but had never seen (193-95). Duniway's journal is also permeated by the heartfelt sorrow evoked by the many disasters the party met with en route. As previously noted, cholera was epidemic that year. Before the Scotts could reach Oregon, Jenny's mother (Anne Roelofson Scott, 1811-52) and her youngest brother, Willie, had both died.

Duniway's experiences made such a long-lasting impression on her that she felt compelled to recreate them in writing again and again. The original trail diary is somewhat terse because the teenaged Jenny rebelliously resisted her father's orders to keep the record as he wished, which meant emphasizing road and weather conditions, but leaving out personal observations. Afterwards, however, she regretted not having written more, and her more intimate thoughts found vent in fictional reinventions of the journey. Her career as a novelist would be repeatedly punctuated by an ongoing reprising of her own westward trek.

The first novel to retell the tale was titled *Captain Gray's Company*; or, *Crossing the Plains and Living in Oregon* (1859), which, although of somewhat dubious literary quality, is honored as Oregon's first commercially published novel. The last novel to reiterate the story was *From the West to the West: Across the Plains to Oregon*, published in 1905. In between, a number of her serialized novels included descriptions of the westward journey taken by a girl or young woman, which was always figured as a profoundly transformative experience.

The joyful bravado displayed by Duniway in the original diary (that seeps through in places despite parental admonitions to keep the account impersonal), such as when she describes the hiking and rock climbing expeditions she and her sisters went on, is found in her fictive recreations of the adventure. We see the thrill of the journey through the eyes of a young girl, liberated from her normally confined existence, and forever changed by that momentary release. She is so enthralled by the vastness of her surroundings that overwhelming heartbreak becomes bearable, and she gains the strength to move on into new territory, both psychic and physical.

After their arrival in Oregon, the newly widowed John Tucker Scott, down on his luck and not in a position to acquire property immediately, decided to try running a "temperance house" (a restaurant/hotel of sorts that did not sell hard liquor), and Jenny, along with her remaining seven siblings, pitched in to help. Her early experience as restaurant and hotel keeper would later be reflected in the entrepreneurial pursuits of several of her fictional heroines, and adds truthfulness to her characterizations.

However, soon after the Scott family took up their new career in Oregon, their lives were rocked by scandal. Jenny's father married a widow who, shortly thereafter, was found to be pregnant by a man other than her previous or current husband, which (given the moral strictures of the day) left the young Scott girls fearing that their own reputations would be ruined by the association (Moynihan 43-50). In the midst of her father's hasty remarriage and its aftermath, Jenny left home and took a job teaching school, which she held until some months later, when she married a prospective farmer, Benjamin Charles Duniway (1830-96). The Duniways occupied two successive homesteads in the following years, the first in an area of Clackamas County, south of Oregon City, which Jenny nicknamed "Hardscrabble." The second homestead, located in Yamhill County, was dubbed "Sunny Hillside."

The new Mrs. Duniway, or Abigail (as we shall occasionally refer to the former Jenny Scott), was not well suited to the life of a farm wife. She complained incessantly, although undoubtedly with good reason, of the never-ceasing tasks allotted to a woman in that unmechanized era—difficulties compounded when her husband put his own needs before hers, and expended their capital buying farm equipment while neglecting improvements to the home. Nevertheless, as she prepared for the birth of her third child, Duniway managed to steal the time to complete her first novel, the aforementioned *Captain Gray's Company*, and her pen had not been completely inactive in the preceding years. In 1857, under the pseudonym of "Jenny Glen," she submitted a poem titled "The Burning Forest Tree" to the *Oregon Argus* for publication.

But poetry was never really Duniway's forte. Her meter was often a bit uneven, and the rhymes somewhat forced, even though a number of her pieces have a good deal of merit, such as "After Twenty Years," written as she traveled across the country in 1872 and revisited the site of her mother's grave, or "Oregon: Land of Promise," written at the same time. (Both were self-published in 1875 in a booklet titled *My Musings*, issued to raise money for her campaign for women's rights, and were also printed in 1876 with her epic poem, *David and Anna Matson*.)

The editor of the *Argus*, William L. Adams, printed Duniway's early poems, but urged that she "could write a very fair prose article, and would suggest that she try her hand on that kind of composition hereafter" (qtd. in Moynihan 19). In the following years, heeding the advice, she contributed items to the *Argus*, and to another publication, *The Oregon Farmer*, a number of which were signed "A Farmer's Wife." These contributions exhibited a dawning feminist consciousness, and she later remembered that "these articles awakened a good deal of rather virulent criticism because of their trenchant excoriation of the way the frontier mothers of growing families were often compelled to toil and slave" ("How I Became").

Loneliness, born out of isolation, along with a burning desire to find something more in life, must have led Duniway to turn her hand to novel writing. However, despite the fact that its author was 25 at the time it was published, it would be kindest to look at her first effort in this direction, *Captain Gray's Company*, as a work of juvenilia. The novels written during the heyday of her career, serialized in the *New Northwest* and *The Pacific Empire*, are so stylistically superior and so much more sophisticated, they almost seem to have come from a different pen. Duniway herself later called her first full-length work a "crude and callow novel" ("How I Became"), and the critics were not kind, either at the time of publication or afterwards.

Captain Gray's Company, as noted, is a fictional recreation of the adventures of the Scott party on the trail to Oregon. In the opening, we meet the widow Goodwin and her three children—Effie, Herbert, and Willie—who decide to go west along with the Gray family after losing their home. The party later takes on additional members, including the Mansfield family. Once across the Missouri, 17-year-old Ada Mansfield and Maurice Stanton, the young doctor she is in love with, make war on the disease ravaging travelers. But despite all efforts, Mrs. Goodwin dies, along with little Willie (as did Duniway's own mother and small brother), leaving Effie and Herbert orphaned, and others of the party also die. Upon reaching Oregon, Effie is forced to work as a domestic in the home of a haughty employer, who is infuriated when her stepson, Hubert, falls in love with her servant, and who tricks him into believing Effie doesn't love him. But meanwhile, Effie's brother Herbert has made good in the gold fields, and comes back with enough money to take Effie out of service and put them both through school. Years pass, and in a classical comic denouement, the wrongly parted lovers are reunited and married in a joint ceremony in which Herbert also marries his true love. In another strand of plot (somewhat loosely related), we find that Ada, who has married Maurice, has made plans to begin publication of an "Oregon Magazine," with her husband's full endorsement. The concluding chapter, titled "Improvement of Oregon Literature," ends with a poem and the remark that "Oregon literature is beginning to look up" (341), making it apparent that one of the author's major goals has been to promote the growth of literature in the new state (which had just been admitted to the union), and she has been so brave as to see her own contribution as a substantial beginning.

The characters of both Ada and Effie vicariously fulfill Duniway's own dreams. Effie gets the education Duniway wishes she had been able to have, and Ada, wealthier than Duniway herself, is in a position to start a literary venture, a fictional forerunner of the *New Northwest*. But the Duniways' fortunes were not fated to parallel those of the author's fictional heroines as closely as she would have liked. The couple did not prosper as farmers, and it would be over a decade before Abigail was able to launch a periodical of her own.

In *The Literary Impulse in Pioneer Oregon* (1948), Herbert B. Nelson charged *Captain Gray's Company* with being a "romantic, sentimental, jumbled account [. . .—] such a confusion of love and marriages that it is meaningless and far too dull to repay the careful reading that would be required to untangle the complicated skein of the plot" (41). And yet, although the criticism of its style seems warranted, one regrets that Nelson apparently did not read carefully, because beneath the flawed prose there is depth to the ideas; it is not merely "silly."

Even though the novel is overly sentimental and full of trite description, it conveys a sense of real experience, heightened by the incorporation of many passages from Duniway's actual trail diary. These are purported to be extracts from the diaries of characters in the story, and the transitions between them and the rest of the narration are somewhat clumsy, but the effect is vivid nevertheless. Furthermore, the novel provides firm evidence of Duniway's awakening feminist perspective. The maltreatment of women is a dominant theme, as is a concern with women's health issues. In a letter to a friend, Duniway's heroine writes:

> I shall laugh, and ride horses, and jump ropes, and climb hills, no matter what prudish matrons may say [. . . .] I would not be unfeminine, but I would be *healthy, active* and *happy*. How sad I sometimes feel, when I reflect upon the way that most American women live! No wonder consumption and debility, and constant suffering are the common lot [. . .]. (281)

In another passage, we are cautioned that marriage leaves a woman vulnerable. "There is a risk to run," admonishes one of Duniway's characters, "when a dependent creature trusts herself, happiness, life, love, everything, in the power of a husband, that few consider properly" (325). All of this suggests that although it would take the author awhile longer to hone her literary skills, she knew what she was aiming for early on, and was rapidly acquiring a mission that would direct the future course of her life.

In the spring of 1862, Ben Duniway, struggling to make a profit as a farmer, left to try his luck in the Idaho mines. In his absence, Abigail tended the children, kept up the homestead, and resumed her career as a school teacher. But Ben was less successful as a miner than as a farmer, and returned in the fall. Shortly thereafter, because of debts Ben had incurred by cosigning on a loan for a friend (against Abigail's advice), Sunny Hillside was sold, and the Duniways moved to a house in Lafayette, Oregon. Abigail continued teaching school, and Ben went to work as a teamster, but he was run over by a wagon pulled by a team of runaway horses, resulting in a back injury that left him permanently semi-disabled.

In 1865, the family moved to Albany, Oregon, where they hoped to recoup their fortunes. Abigail started a school, but soon began to think she might do better by going into business, and in 1866 she opened a millinery store. In her memoirs she recalls that the plights of the women she met in her shop, brought about by unjust laws and customary ideas about women's "proper" behavior, urged her to begin her public campaign for equal rights. In 1870, she founded a State Equal Suffrage Association and planned a newspaper dedicated to equal rights issues (Moynihan 84). The following year, she represented Oregon at a woman's suffrage convention in San Francisco, where she met many leaders of the movement, and underwent an even more thorough transformation.

PUBLISHER & AUTHOR

After returning from California, Duniway decided to take her family to Portland, Oregon, where she founded the weekly *New Northwest*, which she would publish and edit for the next 16 years. By this time, she had borne all of her six children; a daughter,

Clara Belle (1854-86), and five sons—Willis Scott (1856-1913), Hubert Ray (1859-1938), Wilkie Collins (1861-1927), Clyde Augustus (1866-1944), and Ralph Roelofson (1869-1920). However, she did not allow motherhood to hinder her career. With the assistance of her husband and hired domestic help, she was freed to travel extensively, canvassing for the paper, addressing public meetings, and raising support for equal rights, as well as gaining fodder for her editorials and ideas for her novels. In 1871, Duniway invited Susan B. Anthony to come to Oregon. Together, they embarked on a lecture tour of the Pacific Northwest. With the benefit of Anthony's teaching, Duniway would rise to a position of importance in the far west equivalent to that held by her mentor in the east, and would also achieve national fame. After that first tour, she traversed the continent many times to lecture and attend woman's congresses in faraway cities, retracing quickly by railroad the route she had arduously traveled in 1852. Her impassioned oratory made her a much-sought-after speaker in meetings coast to coast, and she served as one of several national vice presidents of the National Woman Suffrage Association (NWSA). But the majority of her time was spent closer to home in her "chosen bailiwick" (Oregon, Washington, and Idaho—the states of the old Oregon Country to which she had journeyed in her youth). The pages of the *New Northwest* contain the bulk of Duniway's literary output, 17 of her serialized novels (as well as a serialized version of the earlier-published *Captain Gray's Company*) and countless columns of editorials.

The Duniway newspaper was a family affair. At home in Portland, Abigail's children assisted in publishing the weekly, learning skills that would help in their later careers. For a time, her sister Kate (Catherine Scott Coburn) served as associate editor. Kate later became an editor of the Portland *Oregonian*, whose chief was brother Harvey Scott. Over the years, Abigail's relationship with Harvey was tempestuous. At times, he adamantly opposed the equal suffrage initiatives she advocated, and because of his enormous clout as director of Oregon's biggest newspaper, he was very influential in the delay of woman's suffrage legislation (Kessler; Nash).

Although during the *New Northwest* years Duniway's writing was almost entirely limited to that which can be found in its pages, in 1876, when she went east to join in the NWSA's protest of the celebration of the nation's centennial, she found a New York publisher for her epic poem, *David and Anna Matson*. It appeared that year in an illustrated volume, along with a number of shorter poems, and was republished in 1881 by the Duniway Publishing Company.

David and Anna Matson is based on a tale told by John Greenleaf Whittier, "David Matson," that Duniway had printed in the *New Northwest* in 1875, which in turn is based on Tennyson's long narrative poem, "Enoch Arden" (1865). Tennyson tells the story of Enoch Arden, who goes to sea and is cast away on a desert island. Eventually he is rescued, but not until his wife, Annie, has given him up for dead and married another, Philip Ray, "a good man, rich and honored." When Enoch returns, he finds out what has happened and goes into hiding so as not to cause further grief, and eventually dies alone. Whittier starts his tale by writing that Tennyson's poem had "reminded me of a very similar story of my own New England neighborhood" (*NNW* 26 Nov. 1875). He then tells the story of David Matson, who leaves his wife Anna and two sons to go to sea on a ship owned by fellow townsman Pelatiah Curtis. The ship is seized by pirates and David is sold as a slave in Algiers, where he remains for several years until he's liberated by an American official. About to leave for home, he meets Pelatiah, who tells David that he's married Anna. David, resigned to his fate, gives Pelatiah a shawl for Anna, which he's bought as a homecoming gift, and remains in Algiers. Pelatiah returns home, and gives Anna the present. She refuses to wear the shawl sent by David, although she has it wrapped around her shoulders on her deathbed.

In somewhat ragged verse interspersed with colloquialisms that jar the generally more elevated tone, Duniway retells Whittier's story, adding some details from Tennyson's lengthier account—but with a slant. In "Enoch Arden," Philip is motivated by genuine love. He generously offers assistance to Annie when she is down on her luck after Enoch goes away. He even sends her children to school. Philip and Annie wait eleven years until they are married, after all hope of Enoch's return has ceased. It is a tender story, a moving tale of self-sacrifice. In Whittier's "David Matson," we never really find out what motivates Pelatiah, although he seems eager to dispose of David when he reappears. Duniway, however, tells the story the way she thinks it is more likely to have happened, knowing how women are taken advantage of by men. She characterizes Pelatiah as a stereotypical miser, a pious hypocrite. Not many years after David is lost at sea, Pelatiah takes advantage of Anna's desperation. After depriving her of all possible sources of income, he tricks her into marrying him. Reluctantly, she does so, although not before trying to mortgage her house to him for money to leave and go find work. But he had refused, claiming that his hands were tied because the law did not allow her, as a woman, to sell "her husband's" land. After their marriage, he treats David's sons shabbily, and won't send them to school. Anna must sneak what she can from her own household money to better their lives. This is a sharp contrast to the generosity of Philip in Tennyson's poem. *David and Anna Matson* will never be remembered for its beautifully crafted lines, but it is a fascinating study in the way authors play upon each others' plots, and shift the meaning in the process. It is also a notable forerunner of the many feminist retellings of narratives originally told from a masculine perspective that became very popular in the last decades of the twentieth century.

By 1886, ten years after the publication of *David and Anna Matson*, Duniway had fallen out with leaders of the woman's movement because of her pro-temperance but anti-prohibition stance on alcohol. The Women's Christian Temperance Union (WCTU) was a rising force, gathering support for nationwide prohibition. Duniway foresaw that such legislation would be ineffectual, but more importantly, she was keenly aware that agitation by women for prohibition would delay gaining voting rights, which had to be granted by male electors. Many powerful men had vested interests in alcohol-related businesses, or did not want any infringement on their own right to drink.

Duniway was vociferous in her denunciation of the prohibitionist element among woman's movement activists. Her detractors claimed that she had "sold out to alcohol," and they made it difficult for her to continue operating. Subscriptions to the newspaper began to fall off. At this time, Duniway suffered a sharp blow when her daughter, Clara, died from tuberculosis. The political tensions, as well as her bereavement and a desire to try to improve the family's fortunes, encouraged Duniway to leave the newspaper business and invest in ranch property in Idaho's Lost River Valley, where mining interest was high and irrigation was bringing agriculture to arid lands.

In 1887 Duniway moved to the family's new ranch in Idaho, but she soon realized that she had made a mistake. Not only were the prospects for getting rich slimmer than she had hoped, but she felt out of her element on a remote ranch, having become accustomed to being in the middle of political action. Also, she was unhappily married. For years, she had regretted her hasty marriage to Ben. She might have considered divorce, but knew that it would create a scandal that would damage her influence, and so merely separated from her husband and returned to Oregon. Except for her occasional visits to the ranch, the couple remained estranged from that time until Ben returned to Portland shortly before his death in 1896.

In 1891, Duniway began a short-lived periodical, *The Coming Century*, but was unable to obtain sufficient financial backing to continue. Then, in 1895, she undertook the editorship of a new weekly, *The Pacific Empire*, published by Portland entrepreneur Frances Gotshall. However, in 1897, frustrated because Gotshall did not have sufficient resources, she resigned.

After this last venture in journalism, Duniway (by then 63) retired from business, although she continued to lecture, head the Oregon State Equal Suffrage Association, campaign for equal rights, and write. In the last years of her life, she revised several of her serialized novels and submitted them to publishers in the east, but without success. Literary tastes were changing, and Duniway's style belonged to the era just past rather than to the modernist trend of the beginning of the twentieth century. She also had to contend with the widespread prejudice of the eastern literary establishment against western writers and western subjects, and a lack of acceptance of her radically feminist politics. However, in 1905 A.C. McClurg of Chicago did bring out her final novel, *From the West to the West*, the last retelling of her 1852 journey to Oregon. This was an attempted revision of *Captain Gray's Company*, and no doubt found a publisher because its semi-autobiographical nature made it attractive on the basis of her personal fame. As she discusses in the preface, she had "yielded to a demand" for republication of the earlier novel, but instead of doing precisely that, wrote *From the West to the West* instead. She explained that

> Among the relics of the border times that abound in the rooms of the Oregon Historical Society may be seen an immigrant wagon, a battered ox-yoke, [etc.]. Such articles are valuable as relics, but they would not sell in paying quantities in this utilitarian age if published and placed upon the market. Just so with "Captain Gray's Company." [. . .] Let it rest, and let the world go marching on. (ix-x)

The story told in *From the West to the West* is vastly different than the tale found in *Captain Gray's Company*. Here, instead of masquerading in the dual personas of Effie Goodwin and Ada Mansfield, she casts herself as a heroic teenage spitfire, Jean Ranger, daughter of John and Annie Ranger (the names used are very similar to the names of the actual Scotts), whose family is an idealized version of Abigail's own.

The Ranger family, headed for Oregon, is joined by Sally O'Dowd, who has left her abusive husband and is escaping to the west with her children (who had been awarded to their father's custody). Along the way, they pick up a runaway slave and her small son whose master (the boy's father) is about to sell them separately, and Mrs. Benson and Mrs. Daphne McAlpin (mother and daughter). Daphne has left her husband, much her senior, whom she does not love but married at her mother's urging. She is also fleeing to the west, where she will seek a divorce. After Annie Ranger's death en route, and the eventual arrival of the group at their destination, John Ranger marries Sally O'Dowd, whose estranged husband has fortuitously committed suicide in the interim (although not before putting in a personal appearance to further complicate the plot). Daphne's husband, Donald, also shows up and agrees to let her go—after facing up to the fact that he had actually been in love with the mother, not the daughter, all along. He admits that he married her merely because society decreed that a younger wife was more desirable. After the divorce, defying convention, Donald marries his ex-wife's mother, and they leave for Europe to escape the gossip that such a switch is bound to provoke! Jean Ranger is united with handsome mountain man Ashton Ashleigh, whom she met during the journey west.

The plot of *From the West to the West* is much more self-consciously feminist than that of *Captain Gray's Company*, and the writing technique, enhanced by the use of such devices as symbolic foreshadowing, is more sophisticated than that of its predecessor. However, Jean's outspoken radicalism is anachronistic; it would take Duniway herself many years after her arrival in Oregon to develop the controversial perspectives voiced by her fictional alter ego at the age of 16. In addition, at this time in her life—perhaps because of depression and illness, along with political frustrations and financial woes—she was no longer writing her best. The appealingly witty, often stingingly facetious narrative voice that she had developed are absent here, replaced by a morbid longing to relive the past as it might have been.

And yet, although Duniway's career as an author was somewhat uneven, and even her best efforts can justifiably be criticized due to the hurried composition resulting from conflicting demands upon her time, her writing is still compelling today. When we read her striking descriptions we can better understand how formerly submissive women found the courage to demand their rights, as well as how circumstances in the American west fostered their success in obtaining them.

By the time of her death 1915, Duniway had seen women win full voting rights in all the states of her "bailiwick"—in Idaho (1896), in Washington (1910), and in Oregon (1912). She wrote Oregon's Equal Suffrage Proclamation in her own hand at the request of governor Oswald West, and was the first woman in the state to register to vote.

NOVELIST WITH A PURPOSE

Abigail Scott Duniway's lively, entertaining, and very persuasive novels are all western melodramas of the type that held widespread appeal for audiences in the closing decades of the nineteenth century. These action-packed narratives, which would play quite well on the stage, are in some respects similar to, but also contrast sharply with male-authored stories set in similar locales. Although her tales use many of the same conventions, the situations are often reversed—strong women rescue their menfolk from trouble, and law enforcers are generally villains because they enforce legislation that robs women of their rights. Like the women writers of popular westerns who would come after, she helped "refine, reshape, and redefine the western to embrace wider frontiers" by introducing "social issues that are relevant to both sexes" (Piekarski 909). And yet, because she did so at an earlier date, she should be rightfully acknowledged as their predecessor, one of the originators of an ongoing tradition in western fiction by women writers.

However, unlike many sensationalistic novels written then and now, Duniway's stories were more intellectual, and rested on clearly articulated ideological underpinnings. They were not created to generate large sales revenues by titillating readers who longed chiefly for thrills or romance (although their plots are packed with adventure and oozing with love). Instead, they were designed to reveal by example the full extent of the effects of women's prolonged lack of power, and to win support for change.

In Duniway's own mind, her serialized novels were her greatest legacy. She predicted that the novels "bound up in the volumes of the *New Northwest*" would be published as her "posthumous contributions to generations yet unborn." She foresaw that future readers would "marvel at the facts therein portrayed as much as the student of today is marveling at the progress of the world since the discoveries of Christopher Columbus, or the explorations of Lewis and Clark." Duniway was careful to add that she had not made this claim in a "spirit of boasting" but merely as a statement of what she believed would become fact. Her prediction was based on an extensive knowledge of literature and history, and on an intuition honed sharp in a long and fruitful public career ("How I Became").

In truth, neither novel discussed earlier has nearly as much fascination or vigor of style as do those composed during the peak of her career as publisher, editor, and campaigner for women's rights—the novels serialized in the *New Northwest* and *The Pacific Empire*. When read with an appreciation of nineteenth-century literary conventions, these tales, heartily sprinkled with their author's ironic and often biting humor (similar to that found in the works of her chief literary idol, Charles Dickens), are as entertaining now as they were for their original readership. A typical example of this style is found in Duniway's 1876 novel, *Edna and John, A Romance of Idaho Flat*, where we read that

> Sometimes love is like leprosy, fastening its virus in the veins of its victim and fettering the subject for life to the chains of a slow consumption of all that was sparkling and hopeful in the better nature previous to the attack. [. . .] Women of experience are the only mortals who should be entrusted with the making of marriage laws. Women when in love, and without the experience that love brings in its train of consequences, are no better qualified to rule the world of motherhood than are the present law-makers, who know no more of the needs of mothers than a goose can know of astronomical trigonometry. (120)

Another characteristic quip can be found in the episodes of *Judge Dunson's Secret*, where we find the wry remark, "It is sadly and strangely true that manly men whose differences in intellectual comprehension can never be made to harmonize upon any other theme have often blended their opinions in regard to the woman question. [. . . each] will agree with the other in the fancy that woman, but for their power over her, exercised by and through the mastery of the law, would at once degenerate from purity into wantonness. That there are legions of honorable exceptions to this self-evident fact [. . .] in no way detracts from the validity of this axiom" (*NNW* 2 Aug. 1883). The pages of Duniway's serials teem with similar amusing, yet serious observations.

More importantly, however, as their author predicted, these novels reveal historical facts that might otherwise be lost to cultural memory. Duniway's bold heroines are forthright in their determination to achieve sweeping goals, and they shatter lingering misconceptions about women's behavior in the nineteenth century. Her novels all served the primary purpose of illustrating the consequences of obeying or disobeying the civil and moral laws that governed the treatment of women in American society. They were meant to teach their audience how and why it was that women were treated like slaves, and what was necessary to bring about change. As the stories unfolded, readers saw that conditions could improve, and were better equipped to put principles into action.

Some have criticized Duniway's novels for their author's sometimes disorganized style of composition—she roamed the country on the campaign trail carrying scraps of stories like "numerous waifs" in her traveling basket, and often composed chapters without having any of the previous ones on hand ("Editorial Correspondence" *NNW* 10 Mar. 1876). As a result, facts sometimes don't jibe, or there is an unevenness in tone and style.

Still, some of the features of Duniway's work are actually typical of most nineteenth-century serialized novels. When subsequent chapters of a book are written and published either weekly or monthly, the complicated plots, which sometimes seem somewhat poorly connected, are as they are because they have evolved over time. Julia Prewitt Brown describes serialized stories as being "a little like long-cooking stews; all the ingredients (or all the main characters and conflicts) are there in the beginning, but they thicken and change in consistency over time, or over the extended length of the serial" (110). To fully appreciate any novel that was originally published in serialized form, one must begin to imagine it from the point of view of its original readers. The hair-raising events found in successive chapters that seem somewhat implausible if read one after the other, seem more palatable when read at intervals.

It would be a mistake to believe that the changes that occur over the course of a serialized novel, and the gaps that we perceive, are necessarily evidence of a fatally flawed structure. On the contrary, these seeming inconsistencies actually often help to create a sense of realism. Reading novels chapter by chapter over a period of many months was a course that "was intertwined with a vision of life no longer shared by the dominant literary culture of the twentieth century" (Hughes & Lund 2). The stories showed how life was a continuous, messy process, but one in which nearly miraculous transformations could occur nevertheless. Seeing how characters progressed over time, readers could easily imagine that the changes seen in fiction could come about in real life.

Although Duniway's narratives have much in common with many American novels by women, including nineteenth-century blockbusters such as Harriet Beecher Stowe's *Uncle Tom's Cabin* (1851), and Helen Hunt Jackson's *Ramona* (1884), the title which can best define all these works is *not* that of "woman's fiction," as discussed by Nina Baym. For Baym, this label describes a type of writing which tells "one particular story about women" (22): in all cases the heroines "change their situation by changing their personalities" (19). Their victories are psychological. But Duniway's novels are much more outwardly directed. They are more plot- and action-centered, and all of her heroines know that, even if they must first change their personalities—become less slavish and more willing to fight for their rights—they must also go out and change the world and the men who currently control it. Neither can we classify Duniway's stories as "sentimental novels" using the definition offered by Jane Tompkins—the most prominent "sentiment" in (or engendered by) Duniway's novels is often sheer rage. Tompkins describes sentimental novels as ones that share a "concern with social issues" and can be read as "training narratives," two traits that give them kinship with Duniway's works. However, she also observes that in these tales the male figure who marries the heroine is "the alternative to physical death [. . . who] provides her with a way to live happily and obediently in this world while obeying the dictates of heaven" (183). This is definitely not the case in Duniway's narratives.

The category into which Duniway's stories best fit is the more inclusive one of "exemplary narrative," a story told to teach a lesson by example. As its name suggests, the main feature of such writing is that it employs an *exemplum*, a tale encapsulated by a narrator's commentary, given as a model on which to pattern one's actions, or to caution a reader against injudicious ones, and to illustrate a moral. This genre has dominated American (and also British) literature since its inception; indeed, works that are no longer viewed as exemplary in nature, because of our present habits of interpretation, were once thought of as belonging to this category. In Duniway's day, even Shakespeare's plays were assessed primarily on the basis of their exemplarity.

"Exemplary narrative" is a category with a long history of its own, beginning (in English) in the thirteenth century, with the introduction of "exempla" into the vernacular sermons that were then coming into vogue. These exempla, or moralized anecdotes, were either "historically true or fictitious, drawn from sources both ancient and contemporary, secular as well as religious" and have long been recognized as "the medieval parent alike of the novel [. . . and] the household fairy-tale" (Owst 149). The use of the exemplum in Christian teaching carries with it a heavy weight of authority, based on Christ's use of parables. Duniway viewed her writing as a part of this exemplary tradition. In her novel, *Laban McShane*, the heroine asserts that "a genuine novel, with moral lessons running through and through it, often contains a history or epitome of human life or times that is far more valuable to the student than the same amount of historical fact" (*NNW* 12 Nov. 1883).

In the Christian tradition, exempla were effective tools in conversion where more learned approaches failed, and were commonly used to end sermons when listeners were weary of hearing the good word (Owst 152-53). They featured homely characters with which an unlettered audience could identify, and they became the basis for popular literary forms—the exemplary biography and autobiography, the novel—that have persisted into the present. In all cases, the lives of particular individuals are viewed as demonstrations (examples, or exempla) of various moral principles. Actions, more than characters (who are often portrayed in somewhat stereotypical fashion) are the driving force of such stories, because the acts—right or wrong—are privileged, and not the particular actor who performs them. The author shows that such actions can/could be performed by other like-minded individuals, and that a successful outcome depends on adhering to the principle being demonstrated, and not on who applies it.

Duniway's exemplary narratives are typical of the genre, and she is expert in this type of artistry. As a result, her novels are effective vehicles for conveying the messages of the woman's movement. Vigorous action is combined with forceful commentary in scenarios which are both familiar and strange—familiar because most men act in the same old high-handed, domineering ways and most women continue to participate in their own enslavement, but different because some dare to do otherwise. When unusual, although not impossible, outcomes were realized in exemplary narratives, readers cheered and began to believe change could occur.

Brief summaries of the twenty novels not already discussed are provided in an appendix for the sake of illustration. Of necessity, the complicated plots have been vastly simplified. Unfortunately, with the exception of *Edna and John, A Romance of Idaho Flat*, none of Duniway's novels have yet been reprinted. They are available only on microfilms of the *New Northwest* and in the few remaining sets of *The Pacific Empire* (although extensive synopses are provided in Jean Ward's dissertation, "Women's Responses to Systems of Male Authority").

The themes of Duniway's novels are the concerns that were most important to her and to the other radical leaders of the early woman's movement. She explores five large issues:

1. **Laws** other than those that excluded women from voting, and religious prejudices that relegated women to a second-class status;
2. **Alcoholism and abusive behavior** and their role in tyrannizing the lives of women, particularly the wives of abusers;
3. **Political tactics**, including dissimulation, required by women to forward their interests in a world dominated by men;
4. **Entrenched definitions of gender roles** that foster the objectification of women and preclude equal-employment opportunities and wages;
5. **Restructuring of society** to create an atmosphere in which women can achieve their fullest potential with the help of cooperative living, day care, and domestic responsibilities shared equally by men and women.

Although these issues appear in combinations in all of Duniway's novels, certain narratives stand out as examples of particular concerns. For instance, in a brief look at *Edna and John*, we find a compelling investigation of the effects of unjust civil laws and religious bias. In the novel, Edna, a naïve young girl, forms a foolish romantic attachment to the thriftless John. Unable to make a living in their native Missouri, they immigrate to Idaho and find themselves in the midst of a gold rush. John falls prey to the dual temptations of gambling and alcohol, while Edna, soon the mother of two, earns the family's living by opening a restaurant. After much hesitating, Edna leaves John but finds that the laws are in his favor. As a wife, she has no claim to her own children or her own earnings, which the dissipated John wastes frivolously. When she tries to get a divorce she is denied by a judge who claims she has no grounds. Religious authority insists that it is her duty to stand by her man, no matter what. The stories of the other female characters in the novel demonstrate additional injustices. Edna's mother, Susan Rutherford, is left a widow, and dower laws deny her the property accumulated through a lifetime of hard labor. Edna's Aunt Judy is deceived in marriage by a man who has left a previous wife back east. When he dies, she is left penniless. It is no wonder that, after a self-righteous judge refuses her request for divorce, Edna starts packing a revolver and decrees, "Men may kill me, or they may compel me to kill them, or myself, but they cannot compel me to longer outrage the laws of God by living a life with my body to which my soul is not true" (165). Likewise, in all of the novels briefly summarized at the end of this booklet, several parallel plots help enhance the themes portrayed in the main plot, and thereby bring the writer's concerns into even greater relief.

There has not been much published commentary on Duniway's novels. Historians examining Duniway's career have tended to gloss over them, or have limited their observations to the connections the tales have to her own life's story. But not recognizing the importance of the novels has led to an undervaluing of Duniway's accomplishments, and not considering fully what they depict about the way in which the early successes of the woman's movement were accomplished leaves the historical record incomplete.

A "THOROUGHLY RADICAL" EDITOR

The slogan emblazoned on the masthead of the *New Northwest* proclaimed that it would be "Independent in Politics and Religion, Alive to all Live Issues and Thoroughly Radical in Opposing and Exposing the Wrongs of the Masses"—an audacious boast indeed for an editor who until recently had been a pioneer farm wife. When the weekly *New Northwest* first appeared, Duniway filled its four very large pages, six columns each, with tightly packed lines of small type containing much more than the average page of the same size. Although it's impossible to determine with certainty which of the many articles without bylines were written by her, we do know that she authored much of the content herself. In addition to her signed editorials and serialized stories, she wrote up column after column of local news, reported on the progress being made on the equal rights front, and added anecdotes gleaned from her day-to-day contacts. As was customary during that era, many of the columns not written by Duniway or her family members (her children also made contributions as they grew old enough to do so) were copied from exchanges with other newspapers across the country, some with credit to the original authors or sources, and some with no credit given at all.

The pages of the *New Northwest* contain the work of such authors as Mark Twain, Fanny Fern, and Bret Harte, letters from Duniway's friend Susan B. Anthony, and offerings by a host of local contributors whose work she encouraged. One notable author whose original work appeared in the *New Northwest* was Frances

Fuller Victor, who sometimes served as substitute editor during the early years of publication. In the late nineteenth century, Victor was recognized chiefly on the basis of her histories, although she was also known for her short stories, which appeared in San Francisco's *Overland Monthly* and *The Golden Era*. But, in addition to the dime novels written pseudonymously in her earlier career, she also produced two longer works of fiction. One was a novella titled *The New Penelope*, and the other a serialized story, *Judith Miles*, which was written for the *New Northwest* in 1873.

Another intriguing figure whose work is found in the *New Northwest* is Minnie Myrtle Miller, wife of the more famous Joaquin. A poet in her own right, she became notorious by going on the lecture circuit to raise money, telling the story of her woes after her husband abandoned her and their children. She had achieved fame as the "Poetess of Coquille" before her marriage, and her verses were published in a number of Oregon periodicals, but the ones that survive are primarily those found in the pages of Duniway's newspaper (Powers).

Duniway's editorials, which were often directly engaged with gender issues, but which also embraced a host of other topics, were frequently very blunt, and she did not shy away from difficult subjects. In a volume titled *"Yours for Liberty"* (after the characteristic way that Duniway signed her name), Jean Ward and Elaine Maveety have published a collection of excerpts from Duniway's editorials that provide an entertaining panorama of her views and do a good job of representing her witty and acerbic style, very much of the same species as that of Twain and others of the Sagebrush School of western journalism. They also reveal something of the nature of the ongoing rivalry she engaged in, western style, with other editors and their newspapers. In one barb, she reports that "A hoodlum 'journalist' makes the startling announcement that Mrs. Duniway's younger children were brought up by hand, as it were, on cow's milk, and considers this a weighty argument against the right of women to the ballot. If the said hoodlum is a specimen of what human milk will do for a child, we are devoutly thankful for the cow" (12 Apr. 1883; Ward and Maveety, *"Yours"* 217-18).

In another column she proudly gives the account of the vigilante-like action taken by a group of about a dozen Washington women against a notorious wife-beater. The women took him from his home, tied him to a fence, and thrashed him. "When the ordeal was gone through with," Duniway reports, "Roberts was warned never again to ill-treat his wife, on penalty of a repetition of the flogging, which he solemnly promised never to do again, and went his way meekly. Good for the women! This is the proper medicine for fellows of his stripe" (26 Nov. 1885; Ward and Maveety, *"Yours"* 258).

In some cases, the scenes depicted in Duniway's "Editorial Correspondence," which were ones she had observed during her travels, can be compared to the descriptions given of the settings of her novels, which were based on what she had seen. For instance, in *Edna and John*, we read of the scene that met Edna upon her arrival in Idaho, featuring a "great desert-like valley stretching afar and anear in all directions with its ash-colored verdure of sage brush, through which wild rabbits roamed, the tortuous Snake and winding Boise Rivers, running like silver ribbons through the distant plain; the mountains, abounding in verdant grasses and gorgeous with floral beauty; [and] the solitary stage making its daily journey through the arid plain" (62). Not long before she wrote those lines, she had described her actual passage through the same locale, during which she found herself "overlooking Boise valley upon one hand, and the great basin, as they term it, on the other." She marveled that "No pen can do it justice. Boise River, and the Payette and Weiser, sparkled like threads of silver among the cloud-mottled shades of the great valley through which they run; and Snake River, like a monster anaconda, wound its tortuous lengths among the far-away foothills as it crawled and surged toward the distant Columbia" (8 July 1876).

In addition to her regular editorials, Duniway also wrote many feature articles on matters of current concern. One particularly important series, titled "The Temperance Problem" (8 July-19 Aug. 1886), details her stand on the prohibition debate, and reveals the nature of the conflict that led up to her selling the *New Northwest*. Washington Territory had recently enacted equal suffrage legislation, and the newly-enfranchised women were seeking to exercise their rights by voting for local-option prohibition laws. Duniway foresaw that such actions would lead to the repeal of woman suffrage in the territory, which did, in fact, come to pass in 1887. Because of her fears, she began a campaign to warn women of the effects of their actions. She didn't mince words, and ended up alienating many former supporters. She cried out that "The temperance agitation as at present conducted is not temperance reform, for it is productive of the wildest intemperance in the thought, speech and action of many of its leaders. [. . .] Its leading agitators, having wandered beyond the pale of reason, are unwilling to accept the honesty of motive that prompts others to take even the most respectful issue with their most impracticable plans or propositions" (22 July 1886). As Moynihan reports, "By the end of 1886 [. . . her detractors] suggested that Mrs. Duniway 'step down' from her work" (147). Although this wasn't the only reason for the sale of the *New Northwest*, as discussed earlier, it was a significant factor.

The Pacific Empire, which Duniway edited between 1895 and 1897, never achieved the fame of the *New Northwest*, but it contributed to the work of the woman's movement in the northwest at an exciting time in its history, during which Utah and Idaho joined Wyoming and Colorado as equal suffrage states. Dedicated to the New Woman of the 1890s, it bore the motto *Alis Volat Propiis*, "She flies with her own wings."

At the time this new journal first appeared, both its editor (Duniway) and its publisher (Gotshall) had high hopes for its success. No large investors were found, and so it would start small— eight pages measuring eight by eleven inches each, plus a yellow outer cover which bore both advertisements and news articles, bringing its size, in effect, to 12 pages total. At the beginning, *The Pacific Empire* was devoted almost exclusively to women's rights issues. In a letter to her son, Clyde, Duniway expressed the desire to turn it into a regular "department journal"—an expansive journal devoted to literary and cultural, as well as political, pursuits (Duniway Family Papers 2 Mar. 1896). These dreams did not materialize. Duniway remained associated with the paper as editor only through February of 1897, and as a contributor through December of that year, when she severed her connections with the enterprise altogether (it ceased publication after July of 1898).

And yet, although her liaison with *The Pacific Empire* had been brief, during the short time she was associated with the publication she wrote the last three of her serialized novels, including *'Bijah's Surprises* (1896; hereinafter referred to as *Margaret Rudson*, which she retitled it when she revised it in 1914). This feminist utopian novel is significant because it preserves the unfulfilled aspirations of its author. *Margaret Rudson* is set on the acreage once owned by Duniway in Idaho's Lost River Valley, which she for a short time called home, and dreamed would be the site of an idealistic venture built along the lines of those depicted in this narrative. Although by 1896, Duniway had given up hope for ever carrying out her plans, she still dreamed.

In *Margaret Rudson*, Duniway imagined a cooperative community formed of emigrants from the crowded cities of the east who, aided by the backing of a wealthy philanthropist, would combine forces to share responsibilities in all areas, including housekeeping and child-rearing, for the betterment of all. The heroine, Margaret, was a typical "New Woman" of the 1890s, freed from the conventions of the past. A wealthy heiress, doctor, inventor, philanthropist, and entrepreneur, she would not even consider marrying her business partner, Silas, until laws were passed enfranchising women and ensuring that, by marriage, she would not lose her rights. Utterly smitten, Silas goes out on the campaign trail, stumping for woman's suffrage, to bring this about, and when they are married, they both take the hyphenated surname, Rudson-Horner, to set an example for other couples in the utopian community they've established.

A discussion of *Margaret Rudson* shows how Duniway's fiction and editorial work are intertwined. After the Panic of '93, there were "prevailing hard times," as described in chapter one of the novel. Even before the panic, Duniway had given her opinion on the general economic situation, and had proposed a variety of schemes for its resolution. She had written of a woman (presumably herself) who had a plan to carry forward a far-reaching "scheme for cooperative housekeeping," but was hindered in the development of the enterprise because of a lack of financial resources (because "that woman has a husband who holds her fortune in his grasp"), and a banking system unwilling to lend large sums of money to a woman in such a position (*NNW* 2 Sept. 1886). This scheme might have been the forerunner of that proposed in *Margaret Rudson*. As Duniway wrote to her son Clyde in 1893, she had long thought deeply about what sort of form American society should take in a future time when equality would reign. She regretted that a wealthy few had given their descendants "a perpetual lease upon the natural advantages of the earth, in the long ago, thereby handicapping the great army of the undermillions" and preventing the "doctrine of the 'survival of the fittest'" from running its course. She went on to say that "individual ownership in land, air and water belongs of right to all [. . .] and their possession should be determined by use and nothing else" (Duniway Family Papers 31 Dec. 1893). It should be noted, however, that Duniway's ideas, although radical, were shared by many during the 1890s, and in ways seemed less radical at the time than they do, in retrospect, today. In the nineteenth century, social reformers of all persuasions founded utopian communities with high hopes for their success. In the United States, the Populist revolt was in full swing, unions were gaining power, and large segments of the population believed that by banding together in cooperative enterprise they could change the balance of power, and break the stranglehold of big businesses.

As she began her editorship of *The Pacific Empire*, Duniway thought she could use the publication to broadcast her views, and maybe even generate enough interest to create a model community designed after her own blueprint. In the first issue, she encouraged readers of limited means to consider combining their capital and labor in order to achieve the success that was "now beyond their reach." She described her vision of "colonies of men and women [. . .] pooling their issues on the corporation plan, for the purchase, equipment and cultivation of the soil, and the possession and enjoyment of independent conditions," and urged discussion of such ideas in the pages of *The Pacific Empire* (16 Aug. 1895). In following weeks (24 Oct.-21 Nov. 1895), Duniway published a series of "Hard Times Talks," which developed plans for a community in which all the members—stockholders—would pool their resources to purchase land and develop homes and cooperative industry upon it. Cooking, laundry, and child care were all viewed as industries, and would be "among the most remunerative of occupations." The result, if these plans had been carried out, would have been a community like the "Utilitaria" found in *Margaret Rudson*, although on a smaller scale, and without the benefit of the capital provided by a single wealthy "altruist" such as Margaret. Although no such community came into being, we have a much better understanding of this editor's career if we consider that this is the direction in which her thought had developed by the time of her retirement from journalism.

PUBLIC VS. PRIVATE SELF

Duniway's *Path Breaking: An Autobiographical History of the Equal Suffrage Movement*, published in 1914, does not provide a very complete picture of its author's life. It was compiled from earlier writings and clippings when she was 80, and nearly on her deathbed—and it was written to fulfill a specific mission. *Path Breaking* was published with the purpose of combating a prohibition amendment on the ballot in Oregon that year, and preventing a "fanatic, church-state coalition," as Duniway termed it, from "affecting the nationwide battle for suffrage" (Moynihan 218). Despite Duniway's efforts, the amendment passed; however, her work to prevent this ultimately ill-fated outcome is not forgotten. The autobiography, which includes two chapters completely devoted to the prohibition issue, leaves an explicit record of her views. "I am opposed to two kinds of prohibition," she writes. "One of these would prohibit woman from the use of her right to vote, and the other would prohibit a man's right to sell a sober man a drink of liquor if he should want to buy." She goes on to compare prohibition to a bandage prescribed to treat an abscess that must be dealt with internally. "The abscess in the Nation's side is drunkenness," she explains. "It is a disease of the Nation's blood; you cannot cure it by sumptuary laws. You must treat it openly, with the sanitary usages of common sense" (100-01).

Path Breaking is a patchwork that wanders from topic to topic, gets lost in nostalgic reverie, and ends with a chapter titled "Mortuary Reminiscences," a melancholy reflection on family and friends who have died. At times its author is too self-congratulatory, and because of her political goal, she is not completely candid. But it's interesting to note that Duniway titled her effort "an autobiographical history of the equal suffrage movement." In doing so, she is by no means claiming that reading the story of her life will explain the entire history of the movement (it would take the compendious *History of Woman Suffrage* by Susan B. Anthony, Elizabeth Cady Stanton, and others to attempt that), but rather, as in her serialized novels, she uses her own life's story (as she uses the stories of her heroines) to demonstrate by example. She shows how her individual efforts, and those of many like her, have combined to bring about dramatic change.

When *Path Breaking* was republished in 1971, historian Eleanor Flexner took her cues in the introduction from what adversaries in the prohibition battle had said. Flexner writes of Duniway's personality (although not of her accomplishments) in an uncomplimentary fashion. She asserts that Duniway's "belief in her own powers and judgment eventually turned into unbridled vanity" and that *Path Breaking* "is the record of an egotist, rendered more so by age" (xi-xii). But this is unjust.

True, "Mrs. Duniway," as she was known, was outspoken and difficult, "noted for her hot temper ever since girlhood" (Moynihan 73). She had such difficulty holding her tongue that it's a wonder she succeeded in politics at all. But she had many staunch friends and supporters, even in her troubled later years. Her correspondence reveals that at the time she wrote *Path Breaking*, she was suffering from the effects of the undiagnosed diabetes that would take her life the following year, when she died of "an infected toe that refused to heal" after the amputation of two others (Moynihan

218). If the letters that she wrote to her son Clyde between 1886 and 1915 were to be published (the only extensive set of her personal correspondence known to exist), her more human side would come into better focus. With Clyde, the child she was closest to after her daughter Clara's early death, she carried on lively intellectual debates, and was not afraid to express plainly her frustrations with her coworkers.

In 1905, when Portland staged a celebration of the Lewis and Clark Centennial, Duniway was the only woman with a special day named after her. That a radical feminist should have been so honored testifies to the great personal esteem in which she was held, and the persuasive power of her writing. On that occasion, she was hailed as the quintessential "pioneer mother." Today this expression summons a picture of a tired woman in a sunbonnet with children on her knees and oxen and wagon in the background. But for Abigail Scott Duniway, such a scene only marked the beginning of a much broader career. There is an enormous discrepancy between the image we have of the heroic but downtrodden pioneer, and the real life of a "pioneer mother" like Duniway. If we wish to recover the missing episodes of the story, we can look to Duniway's personal example, and to her exemplary heroines, and find them.

Appendix

A BRIEF OVERVIEW OF DUNIWAY'S NOVELS

Judith Reid, A Plain Story of a Plain Woman. 12 May 1871 - 22 Dec. 1871. Told in the first person by Judith Reid, now age 50. In her youth, Judith had married a young artist, William Snyder, who had soon after disappeared. After her family moves from Missouri to Oregon, Judith works alongside her father in a sawmill, but after her mother dies she must care for her siblings. She marries a neighbor, John Smith, who treats her badly and will not work. Fed up, she finally returns to Missouri. Luckily, Smith dies, and the long-absent William finally reappears and explains all. They are married, and he is supportive of her in her career as a writer and woman's rights advocate.

Ellen Dowd, the Farmer's Wife. Part one, 5 Jan. 1872 - 26 Apr. 1872. Part two, 1 July 1873 - 26 Sept. 1873. A girl suffers the consequences of an early runaway marriage, which she was driven to because her grandfather tried to force her to marry her much-older tutor. Eventually she dares to seek a divorce and finds success after emigrating to California, where she enjoys her freedom and becomes a wealthy equal rights activist.

Amie and Henry Lee; or, The Spheres of the Sexes. 29 May 1874 - 13 Nov. 1874. After the death of her parents, brought on by her father's abusive treatment of her mother, Amie is forced to take a job in a saloon to support her younger siblings. Although eventually she opens a millinery store, her reputation has been damaged, and her brother Henry, with political aspirations, refuses to associate with her. However, in the end he realizes she has been unfairly treated and becomes an equal rights advocate. Amie goes on to become a successful writer.

The Happy Home; or, The Husband's Triumph. 20 Nov. 1874 - 14 May 1875. On her return from boarding school, Mattie Armstrong finds her father's mistreatment of her stepmother unbearable, as does the stepmother herself, who finally gets fed up and leaves. After this, the father, who is not interested in taking care of the remaining children, sells the family home to Mattie and takes off. Mattie then turns her family of siblings into a working democracy and achieves monetary success. In the conclusion, she marries her long-time suitor, Dr. Amos Harding, believing that because she has achieved financial independence the marriage can be a real partnership, and she will not be in danger of having to assume a subservient role.

Captain Gray's Company; or, Crossing the Plains and Living in Oregon. 21 May 1875 - 29 Oct. 1875. See previous discussion, pp. 14-17.

One Woman's Sphere; or, The Mystery of Eagle Cove. 4 June 1875 - 3 Dec. 1875. After Josiah Carson, a sea pilot, is caught in an explosion off the Washington coast, his wife Abia helps to rescue him and a girl, Rosa Lee, who was a passenger on the ship that blew up. The Carsons take Rosa in and help her to open a store. Abia gives birth to a baby and townsfolk gossip because it seems it was conceived at a time Josiah was out to sea, but we later learn that it is actually Rosa's. In the denouement, we find that Rosa had married an aristocrat, Lord Dunbarton, who was (unknown to her) already married to another, and she had fled and kept her pregnancy secret. But fortuitously, Dunbarton's wife (who had been forced into the marriage by her parents and never loved him) passes away, and he and Rosa are reunited.

Madge Morrison, the Molalla Maid and Matron. 10 Dec. 1875 - 28 July 1876. After emigrating to Oregon from Indiana, young Madge Morrison assumes responsibility for building the family a cabin when her father dies following an accident. Her mother marries a widowered neighbor who succumbs to alcoholism, and Madge marries George Harrison, who immediately begins to mistreat her. She leaves him, walks to Portland, and takes a job as a waiter, disguised as a boy. Some time later, after George is missing and presumed dead, she goes back to her mother's home, helps cure her stepfather of his alcoholism, and gives birth to a child. But George appears alive and abducts their young daughter, after which the girl dies. Madge gets a divorce and enrolls in medical school.

Edna and John, A Romance of Idaho Flat. 29 Sept. 1875 - 15 June 1877. See previous discussion, pp. 32, 35-36.

Martha Marblehead, The Maid and Matron of Chehalem. 29 June 1877 - 8 Feb. 1878. When Martha and her family travel overland to Oregon, Martha's mother dies en route. Shortly thereafter, her father, Major Marblehead, marries a widow, and Martha marries the widow's son, Thomas, just to get away. When her old suitor, Henry Greensborough (whom she believed had spurned her) reappears, she is devastated. Thomas goes to Washington, D.C., with Major Marblehead, who has been elected to Congress. After Martha learns Thomas is having an affair, she sells their farm and moves to Portland, where she purchases a home, but Thomas sues to recover the farm and has Martha thrown out of the house. Finally, they are divorced, but Thomas gets custody of the children, and so she follows them to Montana, where she finds he is leading a dissipated life and has boarded them with a stranger. Martha falls ill, after which her old suitor reappears and helps her recover the children. Martha and Henry Greensborough are married.

Her Lot; or, How She was Protected (later revised in manuscript form as *Ethel Graeme's Destiny*). 1 Feb. 1878 - 19 Sept. 1878. After *Judith Reid*, Duniway's only other novel written in the first person, this compelling story has an atypically dark conclusion. The tale begins in England, where Ethel is tricked into marriage with Gerald, a dashing sea captain, who takes her to Australia. Eventually, they travel to America, arriving at the dawn of California's 1849 Gold Rush with their children. Gerald disappears into the mines, leaving Ethel to make her way by managing a hotel. Gerald reappears and, through his alcoholism, brings Ethel to ruin. This leaving and returning, along with its consequent ill effects on Ethel and the children, repeats itself several times until the couple has lost two homesteads. Readers then find Ethel running an eastern Oregon boarding house, where Gerald is kept in a locked upstairs room after having made repeated attempts on her life.

Fact, Fate and Fancy; or, More Ways of Living than One. 26 Sept. 1878 - 15 May 1879. Grace and Lillie Emerson are sisters who are opposite in every way. Grace is independent, and not eager to be married. Lillie, a romantic, would like to marry right away. But when Alonzo Snowden and John Anders arrive at the Emersons' Oregon home, Grace falls in love with Alonzo. Although her parents have their doubts about him, they marry, and Lillie marries John. After Alonzo's past comes back to haunt him (among other problems, he has abandoned a girl who became pregnant as a result of their relationship), Grace contemplates divorce, but stays on the condition that they take in the child of his illicit union. But the wronged girl's father appears and kills him. Ironically, Grace lives a happy single life with her adopted daughter, but Lillie bears four children in five years, despairs, takes poison, and dies.

Mrs. Hardine's Will. 20 Nov. 1879 - 26 Aug. 1880. Eliza Hardine is in love with John Ingleton, but a family feud separates them, and after Eliza's family emigrates to Oregon, she learns that John has married another. She then marries Peter Tubbs, not knowing that John's wife died soon after their marriage. Fifteen years pass. Eliza leads a rough life, and ends up keeping a boarding house in Portland after the lazy Peter is unable to support them. Finally, she leaves him. Her mother dies and leaves her a large bequest, but Peter steals a large sum from her account, her brother contests the will, and she loses the inheritance. After Peter dies, she writes a book exposing the judicial system's injustice to women, her lost love John Ingleton reappears, and they marry.

The Mystery of Castle Rock, a Story of the Pacific Northwest. 2 Mar. 1882 - 7 Sept. 1882. This very complicated story bears humorous touches of both *The Tempest* and *Jane Eyre*. In it we find a mad son as well as a mad wife in residence in two separate attics (suggesting the multi-generational effects of ill-conceived relationships). Imogen, daughter of Captain Norton, has been raised by surrogate parents on the Oregon coast after being found shipwrecked as an infant. Years pass and a detective, Marcus Woodstock, arrives seeking Imogen, and returns her to her father. Eventually, she is taken to Norton's plantation in Cuba, where she convinces him to free his slaves, and while he goes to sea, assumes management during the transition. But she has fallen in love with Woodstock, and returns to Oregon to find him. There she discovers that he was married to an insane gypsy woman, who finally committed suicide after being locked (for her safety) in an upstairs room. After Imogen gives Marcus a year to remake himself, they marry.

Judge Dunson's Secret, An Oregon Story. 15 Mar. 1883 - 6 Sept. 1883. The "Honorable" Judge Dunson murders his own young son by pulling out all his teeth when the boy complains of a toothache, which drives the mother insane, leading to her death. Dunson's youthful sweetheart, Zuleika Shannon (now a leading feminist), arrives hoping to bring him to repentance. She does so in three personas: as herself at a woman's rights convention, in the guise of an Irish housekeeper, and masquerading as the ghost of the dead wife—haunting Dunson in nocturnal hours, rattling a bag containing the dead son's teeth. Finally, Dunson confronts his dark secret, is won over to the woman's movement, and marries Zuleika.

Laban McShane, A Frontier Story. 13 Sept. 1883 - 6 Mar. 1884. Twins Edith and Hal live with their father, Laban McShane, in rural Washington. Their mother, who had left years ago because of Laban's abuse, is believed dead. Hal, although the poorer student, is sent to college (but flunks out and takes to drink), while Edith is compelled to stay home because of her sex. When a "Mrs. Susan Brown" arrives and takes on the job of housekeeper, she encourages Edith to demand her rights and cures Hal of his alcoholism. Finally, after getting Laban to agree to send Edith to medical school, Susan reveals herself as the long-lost Anna McShane, explaining that after she left she had graduated medical school herself, and had gone to California, where she established a lucrative practice.

Dux, A Maiden Who Dared. 11 Sept. 1884 - 5 Mar. 1885. When Judge Lofty objects to the man that his daughter, Dux, plans to marry, she pretends to run away to spite him. But instead of leaving, she hides in her own home disguised as "Nathan Ducks," supposed brother of her siblings' nanny. Judge Lofty takes on "Nathan" as an office boy and legal trainee, and they debate women's rights issues in their discussions. We later find that Dux's mother, Madeline, who had left the Judge years before because of his abuse (and whom he believed to be dead) has also joined the household incognito to teach him a lesson, in the guise of Susan, the housekeeper. At last Dux and her mother both reveal themselves, the Loftys are reunited, and Dux goes on to become a lawyer.

The De Launcy Curse; or, The Law of Heredity—A Tale of Three Generations. 10 Sept. 1885 - 4 Mar. 1886. Margaret Emerson, living outside of "Nondescript," Oregon, runs away to marry Professor Sunderland Schoolcraft, but he decides not to go through with it when her mother, Emily De Launcy Emerson, arrives and informs him of "the De Launcy curse," which has condemned members of the family to make runaway marriages and go insane. Finally, after many complicated turns of plot in which psychic insights figure prominently and the credibility of spiritualist doctrine is debated, it is discovered that the curse will be removed from the family when a De Launcy descendant marries a Schoolcraft. Free at last to follow their hearts, the lovers are united.

Blanche Le Clerq, A Tale of the Mountain Mines. 2 Sept. 1886 - 24 Feb. 1887. Jack La Fontaine, owner of a wealthy gold mine in Idaho's Wood River District, falls in love with Blanche Le Clerq, the protégée of actress Madam La Fontaine, but she will not marry him until he accepts her career and changes his beliefs about the "proper sphere" for women. As events proceed, we find out that Madam La Fontaine is actually Jack's mother. She had given birth to him after being victimized by a fraudulent marriage, and had left him to be raised by another so that her doubtful reputation would not affect his chances for future success. In the end, she also becomes a mining magnate, and Blanche is married to Jack.

Shack-Locks: A Story of the Times. 3 Oct. 1895 - 26 Mar. 1896. When John Standish leaves on a journey and does not return, his wife, Mollie, is faced with losing their property (a homestead and sawmill in Oregon's Willamette Valley) due to John's gambling debts. She works out a deal to take over management of the sawmill, which she makes profitable, but finds she can't get title in her own name because she is married. To gain control of the property, she gets a divorce. In the end, John returns and Mollie decides to give him a second chance—after he agrees that they will be equal partners.

'Bijah's Surprises **(later revised in manuscript form as** ***Margaret Rudson, A Pioneer Story*)**. Book one, 2 Apr. 1896 - 26 Sept. 1896; Book two, 1 Oct. 1896 - 31 Dec. 1896. See discussion on pp. 37-40.

The Old and the New. 7 Jan. 1897 - 30 Dec. 1897. Tired of the malarial outbreaks on their farms in Illinois, a group of families move to Oregon. Sixteen-year-old Liza Barton is in love with the attractive Dr. Stockwell, but while they are on the trail he is taken by Indians to help with a measles epidemic, and does not return. After arriving in Oregon, she marries 'Liab Jones. Life is hard. Thirty years later, on his deathbed, he confesses that he knew that Stockwell had been released shortly before their marriage, but did not tell her. After 'Liab dies, Stockwell, who has built a successful practice in California, returns to marry Liza.

Selected Bibliography

WORKS BY ABIGAIL SCOTT DUNIWAY

Manuscripts:
Duniway Family Papers. Special Collections. U of Oregon Library, Eugene.

Periodicals edited by Abigail Scott Duniway:
The Coming Century [Portland, OR]. 1891. Oregon Collection. U of Oregon Library, Eugene. 1.1 (2 Dec. 1891).

New Northwest [Portland, OR]. 1871-87. Oregon Historical Society, Portland. Microfilm.

The Pacific Empire [Portland, OR]. 1895-98. Multnomah County Library, Portland. Bound volumes contain: 16 Aug. 1895; 3 Oct. 1895 to 11 Feb. 1897; 10 March 1898 to 23 June 1898. Oregon Historical Society, Portland. Unbound issues include: 3 Oct. 1895 to 11 Feb. 1897; 2 Sept. 1897 to 7 July 1898.

Publications:
Captain Gray's Company; or Crossing the Plains and Living in Oregon. Portland, OR: S.J. McCormick, 1859.

David and Anna Matson. New York: S.R. Wells, 1876.

Edna and John, A Romance of Idaho Flat. 1876. Ed. Debra Shein. Pullman: Washington State UP, 2000.

From the West to the West: Across the Plains to Oregon. Chicago: McClurg, 1905.

"How I Became a Literary Woman." *The Western Lady* [Portland, OR] 1904: 3. Copy in Duniway Family Papers. Special Collections. U of Oregon Library, Eugene.

"Journal of a Trip to Oregon." 1852. *Covered Wagon Women: Diaries and Letters from the Western Trails, 1852*. Vol. 5. Ed. Kenneth L. Holmes and David C. Duniway. 1986. Lincoln: U of Nebraska P, 1997. 39-172.

My Musings. Portland, OR: Duniway, 1875.

Path Breaking: An Autobiographical History of the Equal Suffrage Movement in Pacific Coast States. 2nd ed. Portland, OR: James, Kerns, & Abbot, 1914. Rpt. New York: Shocken, 1971.

SELECTED SECONDARY SOURCES

"Abigail Scott Duniway." *The Woman's Tribune* [Portland, OR; Washington, DC] 28 Oct. 1905: 1, 72.

Anthony, Susan B., Elizabeth Cady Stanton, and Matilda Joslyn Gage, eds. *History of Woman Suffrage*. Vol. 3, 1876-1885. Rochester: Mann, 1886. Vol. 4, 1883-1900. Ed. Susan B. Anthony and Ida Husted Harper. Indianapolis: Hollenbeck, 1902.

Baym, Nina. *Woman's Fiction: A Guide to Novels by and about Women, 1820-1870*. Ithaca: Cornell UP, 1978.

Bennion, Sherilyn Cox. "The *New Northwest* and *Woman's Exponent*: Early Voices for Suffrage." *Journalism Quarterly* 54.2 (1977): 286-92.

Blair, Karen J., ed. *Women in Pacific Northwest History: An Anthology*. Seattle: U of Washington P, 1988.

Boardman, Kathleen. "Paper Trail: Diaries, Letters and Reminiscences of the Overland Journey West." *Updating the Literary West*. Western Literature Association. Fort Worth: Texas Christian UP, 1997. 177-203.

Brown, Julia Prewitt. *A Reader's Guide to the Nineteenth-Century English Novel*. New York: Macmillan, 1985.

Comer, Krista. "Feminism, Women Writers and New Western Regionalism: Revising Critical Paradigms." *Updating the Literary West*. Western Literature Association. Fort Worth: Texas Christian UP, 1997. 17-34.

Duniway, David C. Introduction. "Journal of a Trip to Oregon." *Covered Wagon Women: Diaries and Letters from the Western Trails, 1852*. Vol.

5. Ed. Kenneth L. Holmes and David C. Duniway. Lincoln: U of Nebraska P, 1997. 21-38.

Edwards, G. Thomas. *Sowing Good Seeds: The Northwest Suffrage Campaigns of Susan B. Anthony.* Portland: Oregon Historical Society P, 1990.

Flexner, Eleanor. *Century of Struggle: The Woman's Rights Movement in the United States.* Cambridge: Belknap, 1959.

——. Introduction. *Path Breaking: An Autobiographical History of the Equal Suffrage Movement in Pacific Coast States.* By Abigail Scott Duniway. 1914. New York: Schocken, 1971. vii-xviii.

Holmes, Kenneth L. Introduction. *Covered Wagon Women: Diaries and Letters from the Western Trails, 1852.* Vol. 5. Ed. Kenneth L. Holmes and David C. Duniway. Lincoln: U of Nebraska P, 1997. 13-17.

Hughes, Linda K., and Michael Lund. *The Victorian Serial.* Charlottesville: UP of Virginia, 1991.

Kessler, Lauren. "A Siege of the Citadels: Search for a Public Forum for the Ideas of Oregon Woman Suffrage." *Oregon Historical Quarterly* 84 (1983): 117-50.

Morrison, Dorothy Nafus. *Ladies Were Not Expected: Abigail Scott Duniway and Women's Rights.* New York: Atheneum, 1977.

Mosher, Joseph. *The Exemplum in the Early Religious and Didactic Literature of England.* New York: Columbia UP, 1911.

Moynihan, Ruth. *Rebel for Rights: Abigail Scott Duniway.* New Haven: Yale UP, 1983.

Nash, Lee. "Abigail versus Harvey: Sibling Rivalry in the Oregon Campaign for Woman Suffrage." *Oregon Historical Quarterly* 98.2 (1997): 134-63.

Nelson, Herbert B. *The Literary Impulse in Pioneer Oregon.* Corvallis: Oregon State College, 1948.

Owst, G.R. *Literature and Pulpit in Medieval England: A Neglected Chapter in the History of English Letters & of the English People.* Rev. ed. New York: Barnes & Noble, 1966.

Piekarski, Vicki. "Women Writers of Popular Westerns." *Updating the Literary West*. Western Literature Association. Fort Worth: Texas Christian UP, 1997. 898-915.

Powers, Alfred. *History of Oregon Literature*. Portland: Metropolitan, 1935.

Scott, Harvey. *History of the Oregon Country*. 6 vols. Vol. 3. New York: Cambridge UP, 1924.

Shein, Debra, ed. *Edna and John, A Romance of Idaho Flat*. By Abigail Scott Duniway. 1876. Afterword by Debra Shein. Pullman: Washington State UP, 2000.

—. "'No Canada for Fugitive Wives': Five Novels by Abigail Scott Duniway, Voice of Equal Rights." Diss. U of Oregon, 1998.

—. "Not Just the Vote: Abigail Scott Duniway's Serialized Novels and the Struggle for Women's Rights." *Oregon Historical Quarterly* 101.3 (2000): 302-27.

Solomon, Martha M., ed. *A Voice of Their Own: The Woman Suffrage Press, 1840-1910*. Tuscaloosa: U of Alabama P, 1991.

Tompkins, Jane. *Sensational Designs: The Cultural Work of American Fiction, 1790-1860*. New York: Oxford UP, 1985.

Victor, Frances Fuller. "Literature." *History of Oregon. Vol. II. 1848-1888. The Works of Hubert Howe Bancroft*. 39 vols. San Francisco: The History Co., 1883-90.

—. "The New Penelope." 1877. *Women of the Gold Rush: "The New Penelope" and Other Stories*. Ed. Ida Rae Egli. Berkeley: Heyday, 1998. 1-68.

Ward, Jean M. "Women's Responses to Systems of Male Authority: Communications Strategies in the Novels of Abigail Scott Duniway." Diss. U of Oregon, 1989.

Ward, Jean M., and Elaine A. Maveety, eds. *Pacific Northwest Women 1815-1925: Lives, Memories, and Writings*. Corvallis: Oregon State UP, 1995.

—, eds. *"Yours for Liberty": Selections from Abigail Scott Duniway's Suffrage Newspaper*. Corvallis: Oregon State UP, 2000.